The Best Advice for Actors

DOUGLAS VERMEEREN

iUniverse

THE BEST ADVICE FOR ACTORS

iUniverse books may be ordered through booksellers or by contacting:

iUniverse
1663 Liberty Drive
Bloomington, IN 47403
www.iuniverse.com
844-349-9409

ISBN: 978-1-6632-6541-8 (sc)
ISBN: 978-1-6632-6542-5 (e)

Print information available on the last page.

iUniverse rev. date: 08/05/2024

INTRODUCTION

Ever since deciding that I wanted to be an actor I have kept journal of inspiring quotes from other actors. Why did I chose to keep a collection of these inspiring quotes? At first they were just thoughts that I agreed with or thought shed light on to who I wanted to become in my own acting career or ideas that I wanted to emulate.

Soon as I gained more experience as an actor in the films and television world I began to realize that this can be a very difficult journey. These quotes and thoughts became much more valuable to me. I began to see how so many of the people I admired had also struggled and gained some valuable wisdom along the way.

As an actor there are many competitive and ultimately discouraging moments. Often for completely unexplainable reasons things don't work out. If you have been an actor or involved in this industry for any length of time you know what I am talking about. You have no doubt had situations like this.

There is absolutely no explanation sometimes why they don't pick you for a specific role. It's not always the best looking, most talented, prepared or most suitable person that gets the job. There are so many factors that go into becoming a working actor that it's almost impossible to describe or predict.

There is no explanation why some performances don't land with an audience. (And to be frank why some performances do.) I recently had a show that I was part of that I didn't like. In fat, when I first saw it I was quite embarrassed. But I was in total disbelief when I went to the public screening and found the audience was absolutely in love with it. The film still rubs me the wrong way, yet people tell me of their love for this film. Again I cannot explain this. (And by the way the opposite has also happened where I loved a project and I have been the only one that did. - Maybe I'm just weird. But again this is such a strange business to predict.)

Maybe that's when the quotes that I have collected became more valuable to me. Some of them are anchors for me. These are words of encouragement to remind me that even the greatest actors before me struggled and that these quotes often gave me a glimpse into their experiences of how they were able to keep going in tough times. These thoughts also remind me that I probably have a lot more in common with the actors I have admired than I have realized. You probably do too.

As you read through these quotes I hope you they will be a source of power and inspiration to you too. I sincerely hope that you will gain strength to stay the course and follow your dreams as you think about these quotes and thoughts.

In some cases these thoughts have also served to help me to look at my approach to acting in different ways. They have also helped me to see myself as a constant learner, with more potential and much more to learn. I am pleased to report that several times these reminders about the art of acting have also helped me to be courageous and bold enough to try new and daring things. Sometimes those moments of boldness really worked out well.

I can remember one occasion where I wasn't quite feeling ready for an audition. I don't think I've ever met an actor yet who really likes the audition process. Sometimes it's quite easy to feel uneasy. Especially when you think of all of the other talented people competing for the some role. Some of these people you may even know and their level of talent could be very intimidating. Needless to say, on this occasion I was almost feeling that there was no point to even showing up at the auditor. In my mind I had already decided that I didn't stand a chance and there was no point to waste anyones time. I was on the verge of cancelling and making some excuse. But just at that moment I found one of my favorite quotes in this book:

You're not going there to get a job.
You're going there to present what you do.
- Bryan Cranston

I began to think about all of the people that would love to be given the privilege to audition. I had that opportunity to present what I do. As I thought about this thought/quote again and again. I decided that my job now was not an audition, but rather to present my version or interpretation of this character. I could do it in whatever way I thought best and whatever way I found interesting.

I decided instead of focusing on my fears I would focus on my choices with this character. I decided to go really bold and really color outside the lines. I had nothing to lose after all.

You are probably thinking that the happy ending to this story is that I got the role. Actually I did not, I was almost instantly told when I came in the room that I didn't have the right look. But a few days later I got a phone call to come back for a second character and that one I got. I blame that entire success on one of the quotes you are about to read.

I have also been impressed by how many of these quotes and thoughts reminded me of how important preparation can be. The art of acting is truly an art that grows with insight and experience. The more we can learn about this sacred craft the higher the levels are that open to us.

I suppose one of the more powerful reminders that these quotes have given me is to remind me that those talented people that I have admired from afar are also human. It is very easy to place those we admire in a different realm far away from our own experience. As I have met and worked with many of my heroes it has been refreshing to see that the levels they have reached are also accessible to me and you if we are willing to continue to work hard and pursue our dreams. The quotes I have shared here have also given me that same hope.

I hope you enjoy what I have shared here and if you enjoyed these I am pretty sure that I will compile a second volume of similar thoughts. I am always collecting these and finding power in them. So keep an eye out.

I hope that these inspirational thoughts will make a difference for you and that you will continue to chase your dreams. Life is short and you only get one chance to create the life you want. From one actor to another I am sure you already have experienced the excitement that this wonderful career can bring to you. I challenge you to really go for it and if these thoughts help you in any way I will be glad and consider this volume a success.

As you read through these quotes you'll notice that haven't put them in any particular order. They are not listed by author in some alphabetical order, nor have they been organized by subject. This book is also not designed to be read from cover to cover although you may do that if you wish.

It has been designed to be similar the journal which I personally use. Whenever I feel the need for inspiration I simply pick it up and start randomly browsing and interestingly enough I always seem to find exactly what I am looking for. I hope you have the same experience.

So with these things in mind I encourage you to get started and see what you can find that will help you right now. I hope you find inspiring thoughts from some of your favorite stars.

Best of luck!
And I look forward to seeing your work in the future!

Douglas Vermeeren

Instagram: @douglasvermeeren
IMDb: Douglas Vermeeren

I feel like everything you learn as an actor growing up is wrong. You're supposed to hit your mark, find your light and know your lines. Those are all things that just make things wooden, dull and boring. - Joaquin Phoenix

I had to stop going to auditions thinking, "I hope they like me." I had to go in thinking I was the answer to their problem. - George Clooney

I don't have to be perfect. All I have to do is show up and enjoy the messy, imperfect, and beautiful journey of life. - Kerry Washington

I don't think dreams die - I think that people give up. - Tyler Perry

Acting is not about being someone different. It's finding the similarity in what is apparently different, then finding myself in there. - Meryl Streep

When I was younger I would go to auditions to have the opportunity to audition, which would mean chance to get up there and try out my stuff, or try out what I learned and see how it worked with an audience. - Al Pacino

As artists, when you have people who care about what you do, I think you should care about those people who care about what you do and give them really cool interactive experiences to make them feel appreciated. - Zachary Levi

Confidence is everything in this business. - Reese Witherspoon

The thing about acting, int's so seductive. You get drawn into a role... it's like a love affair. - Jessica Lange

That's what great about the arts. Everything inspires you. Andy get a chance to grow from watching other people and how they do their work. - Jamie Foxx

You can't make the audience fall in love with a character you don't like. - Kate McKinnon

Acting is about finding the truth within whatever world you're in. - Karen Gillan

You're not going there to get a job. You're going there to present what you do. - Bryan Cranston

It's what still excites me most about acting: letting your imagination go places its never been before. There's nothing better than that. - Robin Wright

That's what acting is. It's about having the courage to allow your audience into the private moments of your characters' lives. - Kerry Washington

As a working actor all I want to do is work. That's it. It's terrifying when you don't work. It's very hard when you don't have work. There have been times when I've been out of work for six months. - Sandra Oh

I realized the more fun I had, the more relaxed I was working, the better I worked. - Bill Murray

You can't be trying to achieve success of any kind in this business without accepting that there's going to be a flip side to it. - Jennifer Garner

---

You can't be that kid standing at the top of the water slide overthinking it. You have to go down the chute. - Tina Fey

---

Acting is not words. Holly Hunter didn't speak in the piano (1993) and she won an Oscar. - Monica Belluci

---

I love acting because it's empowering. It empowers me. - Bryan Cranston

---

If you're an actor, always be true to your character. If you're not an actor, have character and always be true to yourself. - Robert De Niro

---

I knew an actor's career goes up and down and back up again. Your standing in this business can't be your whole identity otherwise your doomed. - Lisa Kudrow

---

Here's your opportunity, now you'v got to make something of it. - Chris Hemsworth

I always tell actors when they in for an audition, don't be afraid to do what your instincts tell you. You may not get the part, but people will take notice. - Robert De Niro

It takes a lot of time and a lot of energy and a lot of focus and dedication to do a film. And it's just not worth it if you're going to be miserable even for a day. - Brie Larson

Between 'action' and 'cut,' that's mine. No matter how big the production is. That's still my space. That's a sacred space. - Oscar Isaac

I want to work with great filmmakers and great actors and get better as an actor. - Bradley Cooper

If it wasn't hard, everyone would do it. It's the hard that makes it great. - Tom Hanks

I personally think if something's not a challenge there's no point doing it because you're not gonna learn much. - Cillian Murphy

I went from years of honing my craft to sudden recognition. It was quite a life changer. - Kathy Bates

---

The simple act of paying attention can take you a long way. - Keanu Reeves

---

Make bold choices and make mistakes. It's all those things that add to the person you become. - Angelina Jolie

---

I can't say I've ever finished a film and been particularly thrilled with myself or patted myself on the back, and maybe that's what's kept me going,. And that's a good thing. It speaks volumes about how I perceive myself. - Ryan Reynolds

---

The art of acting is not to act. Once you show them more, what you show the, in fact, is bad acting. - Sir Anthony Hopkins

---

I think fear is one of the most natural states of most actors. - James McAvoy

You need to know what to do when the sun is not shining. - Robert Downey Jr.

I worked in restaurants the first half of my life. - Bradley Cooper

---

You get what you give. What you put into things is what you get out of them. - Jennifer Lopez

---

Acting is a constant learning process. I strive to improve my craft with each project and never stop growing as an actor. -Reese Witherspoon

---

Acting is a process of relaxation actually. Knowing the text so well and trusting that the instinct and the subconscious mind, whatever you want to call it, is going to take over. - Anthony Hopkins

---

Acting is everybody's favorite second job. - Jack Nicholson

Whatever character you play, it gives you the chance to expose another side of yourself that maybe you've never felt comfortable with, or never knew about. - Laura Dern

Whatever character you play, remember they are always doing something. They are not just talking. They re alive: Going through a drama in which they will go through some sort of dramatic human experience. - Tom Hardy

I never got into this business thinking I'd be live movie star. - Glenn Close

As an actor, you most often play relatively average parts. So to get to play the extreme versions of anything, those are the most exciting parts. - Neil Patrick Harris

I'm just an actor. And if I can leave something behind that my kids will be proud of, then that's what I want. I don't my kids to be embarrassed by anything I've done. - Johnny Depp

The reason actors, artists, writers have agents is because we'll do it for nothing. That's a basic fact - you gotta do it. - Morgan Freeman

I love performing and pretending. It's very easy for me. - Jamie Lee Curtis

I have had so many bad auditions. - Ethan Hawke

Acting is great... the ability to express yourself completely is the most wonderful feeling in the world. Each film is a chapter in my life wherein I learn so much more about myself. - Jennifer Connelly

I don't think enough people admit that there's just something fun bout being in front of people. And that's not a self-centred egotistical thing. - Timothee Chalamet

One of the things about acting is it allows you to live other people's lives without having to pay the price. - Robert De Niro

We actors, we're a fragile bunch, and yet we need to be strong because 90% of our lives is rejection. - Sandra Oh

My Very first audition was on the lot of Paramount. And I was put on tape and it was very nerve-racking. I think it was about 15 pages. - Hailee Steinfeld

I Turned my guest house into this little studio. And we have actors come over and do readings. - Jeff Goldblum

The thing about performance, even if it's only an illusion, is that it is a celebration of the fact that we do contain in ourselves infinite possibilities. - Daniel Day Lewis

As an Actor, what's interesting is what's hidden away beneath the surface. You want to be like a duck on a pond - very calm on the surface, but paddling away like crazy underneath. - Alexander Skarsgard

Theater has given me a different perspective on the way I approach films. - Jake Gyllenhaal

I'm always attracted to lower budget. Not because it's lower budget, but because they tend to be better scripts. - Helena Bonham Carter

The theater, for me, has always become a place where I'm free to be more creative. A place to sharpen my tools. - Ethan Hawke

If you risk nothin, then you risk everything. - Geena Davis

So long as I'm a working actor, I can improve. I want to work with people that frighten me and excite me. And characters that I don't believe I'm the best person for the part. But I'm still gonna try anyway. - Anne Hathaway

Failure is a natural part of life. - John Malkovich

You learn more from getting your butt kicked than getting it kissed. - Tom Hanks

Being a day player is one of the hardest things you can do as an actor. - Bryn Cranston

I have the cliche 'struggling actor' story. I was waiting tables in New York and went out to LA soon after graduation to get some jobs. But it didn't work out. - Pedro Pascal

There's not reason to have a plan B because it distracts from Plan A. - Will Smith

I was afraid of being a failure, of not having the best time or of being a chicken. But every year I get older I think, what was I fearing last year? You forget. And then you move on. - Sandra Bullock

There is a need for aloneness. Which I don't think most people realize for an actor it's almost having certain kinds of secrets for yourself that you'll let the whole world in on only for a moment when you're acting. - Marilyn Monroe

I held down as many jobs as I could find from being a waiter to working at a yoga studio and asa ticket-taker at a small theater company. Anything that would allow me to go out and do auditions. - John Krasinski

Acting spooks me in a good way. - Matthew McConaughey

Perhaps I'm not a good actor, but I would never be even worse at doing anything else. - Sean Connery

It was only when I realized how actors have the power to move people that I decided to pursue acting as a career. - Cate Blanchett

You've got to keep taking certain risks, because my priority is in acting. It's not in movie stardom. - Gary Sinise

I think it's na actor's responsibility to change every time. Not only for himself and the people he's working with. But for the audience. If you go out and deliver the same dish every time… It's meat loaf again… You'd get bored. I'd get bored. - Johnny Depp

Our dream as actors is to tell interesting stories about interesting people. - Eddie Redmayne

On stage you need to emphasize every emotion. But on screen, you need to tone everything down and make it believable. - Tom Holland

Every character has their reasons - even the characters who do dumb things. - Zoe Saldana

For every successful actor or actress, there are countless numbers who don't make it. The name of the game is rejection. You go to an audition and you're told you're too tall or you're too Irish or your nose is not quite right. You're rejected for your eduction, you're rejected for this or that and that's really tough. - Liam Neeson

If you got a good imagination, a lot of confidence and know kind of know what you're saying, then you might be able to do it. I know a lot of colourful characters at home that would make great actors. - Jason Statham

Let's embrace being not normal. - Angelina Jolie

Success isn't always about greatness. It's about consistency. Continent hard work leads to success. Greatness will come. - Dwayne Johnson

Never confuse the size of your pay check with the size of your talent. - Marlon Brando

Making movie is not rocket science. It's about relationships and communication and strangers coming together to see if they can get along harmoniously, productively and creatively. - Julia Roberts

Respect your efforts, respect yourself. Self-respect leads to self-discipline. When you have both firmly under your belt, that's real power. - Clint Eastwood

People ask, 'what's eh best role yo've ver played?' The next one. - Kevin Klein

The performances I enjoy are the ones that are hard to read or ambiguous or left-of-center because it makes you look closer and that's what humans are like - quite mysterious creatures, hard to pin point. - Emily Blunt

As an actor you can do what you want with your role. That's why they hire you. To take the role and make it real. - Ice-T

The idea of exploring character relations and their development over a decade has to be appealing for any actor who cherishes his craft. - Vin Diesel

Work hard to achieve integrity in your work and your relationships with the people you work with. - Rebel Wilson

Your internal dialogue has got to be different from what you say. In film hopefully that registers and speaks volumes. It's always the unspoken word and what's happening behind someones eyes that makes it so rich. - Viola Davis

A voice is a such a deep, personal reflection of character. - Daniel Day-Lewis

I love more than anything looking at a movie scene by scene and seeing the intention behind it. It allows you to really appreciate the hand of the filmmaker. - Jodie Foster

It's simple. You get a part. You play a part. You play it well. You do your work and you go home. And what is wonderful about movies is that once they're done they belong to the people once you make it. - Denzel Washington

Every journey starts with fear. - Jake Gyllenhall

I never act my character - I am them. - Drew Barrymore

As an actor your motives and your own crazy psyche is really all you're responsible for in the movie. - Kate Beckinsale

I think it's aways very important to be comfortable and just kind of expressive. - Zoe Kravitz

There's nothing like getting yourself into character and seeing a different person. It really wears on your vanity. - Elisabeth Moss

It was only when I realized how actors have the power to move people that I decided to pursue acting as a career. - Cate Blanchett

I love acting because it's a bit of an escape. It gives you the ability to reinvent yourself. They say that acting is the shy man's revenge. - Hayden Christensen

One of the weird things about Hollywood is we're all imposters. We're all just gleamed up. - James McAvoy

Age doesn't mean anything. Age doesn't mean can't work as hard. Age doesn't mean I can't do as well as everyone else. - Zendaya

Sometimes opportunities float right past your nose. Work hard, apply yourself, and be ready. When an opportunity comes you can grab it. - Julie Andrews

You've got to think of the audition as an opportunity. An audition's an opportunity to have an audience. - Al Pacino

With the acting, it's somebody else's brainchild. And I'm just sort of helping flesh it out. - Jack Black

I started doing community theatre as a way to make friends. And that was when I caught the acting bug. - Christina Hendricks

I was single-minded on what I wanted to do since I was like nine or ten. - Sam Elliott

Be thankful for the hard times, for they have made you. - Leonardo Dicaprio

I respect the gods f film. - Russell Crowe

I learned that you can't have any expectations with life. You never know what's going to happen. - Jennifer Lawrence

The fun stuff comes when someone is not so strict on sticking to the script. You're allowed the spontaneity and great moments can happen. - Jennifer Anniston

I'm just trying to give the best human expression that I can to any particular genre, which could be comedy, could be drama, could be horror, could be thriller. - David Harbour

There's nothing like getting yourself into character and seeing a different person. It really wears on your vanity. - Elisabeth Moss

I've always considered myself to be just average talent and what I have is a ridiculous insane obsessiveness for practice and preparation. - Will Smith

When you're making a film you become incredibly close. It's not like your filing papers. You're creating with human emotions, so you become very connected, it's familiar and romantic. - Thora Birch

I believe there's an inner power that makes winners or losers. And the winners are the ones who really listen to the truth of their hearts. - Sylvester Stallone

Being polite and grateful will make people more inclined to help you. And if people are willing to help you, you may accidentally get something you want. - Jason Sudekis

I haven't really decided to be an actor yet. I started doing plays when I was about 15 or 16. I only did it because my dad saw a bunch of pretty girls in a restaurant and he asked them where they came from and they said drama group. He said, 'Son, that's where you need to go.' - Robert Pattinson

Your job as an actor is to piece together whatever you've learned in your training or whatever you have in your experienced in your life to piece together a person. - Viola Davis

---

I'm just an ordinary person who has an extraordinary job. - Julia Roberts

---

Do you want to be an actor or do you want to be a celebrity? I made that decision when I went to Juilliard. I wanted to be an actor. So if, I get the opportunity to be an actor and do some cool, fun and interesting projects, I'm going to do that. - Anthony Mackie

---

I'm an artist. Artists don't need permission to work. Regardless of whether I'm acting or not, I write. I write when Im tired because I believe your most pure thoughts surface. - Chadwick Boseman

---

Never worry about bad press. All that matters is if they spell your name right. - Kate Hudson

---

Sometimes you can have the smallest role in the smallest production and still have a big impact. - Neil Patrick Harris

Timing is very important. Words can only have a positive impact on others if they are ready to listen. - Christopher Reeve

As an actor it's easy to be self-critical, saying to yourself 'am I good enough? Am I good looking enough? Am I smart enough?' - Chris Pine

Luck? I don't know anything about luck. I've never banked on it and I'm afraid of people who do. Luck to me is something else: Hard work and realizing what what is opportunity and what isn't. - Lucille Ball

I never planned to win an Oscar. When I auditioned for 'Ray' I was just thinking what a great project it would be. - Jamie Foxx

I went through this realization that acting, at it's heart, is the ability to manipulate your own emotions. - Scarlett Johansson

I know very little about acting. I'm just an incredibly gifted faker. - Robert Downey Jr

Film wise, I invariably look at my work and reckon I could have done it better. I'm also conscious that I'm in a profession where we get more praise than we should compared to the usefulness of what we do. - Jeremy Irons

---

90% of how you learn is watching great people. When you are surrounded by good actors it lifts your performance. - Natalie Portman

---

Anytime you take on a character, you just have to find the parts of the character that you can understand. - Chris Pine

---

If you are safe about the choice you make, you don't grow. - Heath Ledger

---

Our dream as actors is to tell interesting stories about interesting people. - Eddie Redmayne

---

We're so complex. We're mysteries to ourselves. We're difficult to each other and then storytelling reminds us we are all the same. - Brad Pitt

Ultimately you have to not worry about people thinking you should have played him differently. You're the one playing the part so it has to be yours. - Ewan McGregor

We all have a gift. We all have a passion. It's just about finding it and going into it. - Angela Bassett

I wanted to surround myself with people who I think are better than I am, whether they are actors or directors or producers, so that I could learn from them. - Mila Kunis

Sometimes acting is really cool because it forces you to exercise certain muscles that you wouldn't normally be called upon in life. - Jenna Fischer

Our job as actors is to just try to be as accurate and as mindful of what they audience is going through and receiving and processing. - Jason Bateman

It's the actors who are prepared to make fools of themselves who are usually the ones who come to mean something to the audience. - Christian Bale

I've always had the same principle for choosing roles, which is to try and make movies that I would pay to see. - Scarlett Johansson

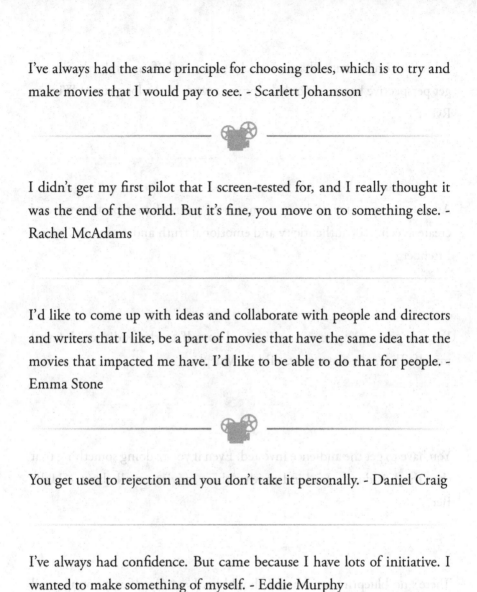

I didn't get my first pilot that I screen-tested for, and I really thought it was the end of the world. But it's fine, you move on to something else. - Rachel McAdams

I'd like to come up with ideas and collaborate with people and directors and writers that I like, be a part of movies that have the same idea that the movies that impacted me have. I'd like to be able to do that for people. - Emma Stone

You get used to rejection and you don't take it personally. - Daniel Craig

I've always had confidence. But came because I have lots of initiative. I wanted to make something of myself. - Eddie Murphy

The most important thing in anything you do is always trying your hardest. Because even if you try your hardest and it's not as good as you hoped you will still have the sense of not letting yourself down. - Tom Holland

I think it's important to have as much as a normal life and take the time to get perspective because it only helps your work in the long run. - Winona Ryder

As an actor you try to bring as much of yourself to a part to try and create a feeling of authenticity and emotional truth and resonance. - Jesse Eisenberg

I'm not performing anymore. I reveal myself to the audience. I reveal myself. That's the show now. - Eddie Murphy

You have to get the audience invested. Even if you're doing something that they think is dumb. It's kind of what these movies are all about. - Halle Berry

There's no blueprint for where I should be. I see myself as a young good actor who still has a lot to learn. There's nobody at any point in their career who is the finished article. - Daniel Radcliffe

Wanting to be an actor and wanting to be famous are different. - Blake Lively

You can only yourself. And it sounds cheesy, but when it comes to filmmaking, there's really nowhere to hide. - Ryan Gosling

---

When you're making movies you've got to get obsessive. - Daniel Craig

Time goes on. So whatever you're going to do, do it. Do it now. Don't wait. - Robert Di Nero

---

If you are going to survive in business, show business or any other business, then you have to be Bold. - Rebecca Ferguson

The best thing an actor can be is ready, be flexible, be ready. - William Dafoe

---

I like working all the time. I hate taking breaks. I don't like weekends. - Joaquin Phoenix

Embrace your differences and the qualities about you that you think are weird. Eventually, they're going to be the only things separating you from everyone else. - Sebastian Stan

All you have to remember is that 'audition' is synonymous with with 'opportunity.' I mean, if you absolutely hate auditioning, do you also hate opportunities? That wouldn't make much sense. - Hiliary Swank

Do something everyday that makes you feel like an artist. Work on your own perspective. - Tom Hiddleston

Acting is a personal process. It has to do with expressing your own personality, and discovering the character you're playing through your own experience - so we're all different. - Sir Ian McKellan

Wanting to be a good actor is not good enough. You must want to be a great actor, you just have to have that. - Gary Oldman

Acting is all about finding the truth within whatever world you're in. - Karen Gillan

Someone said I wasn't attractive enough, people say those things, but they make you stronger. Then you win an Emmy and think, ha ha ha. - Allison Janey

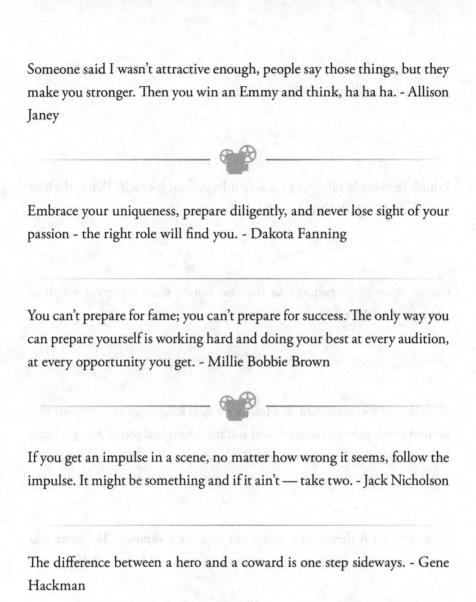

Embrace your uniqueness, prepare diligently, and never lose sight of your passion - the right role will find you. - Dakota Fanning

You can't prepare for fame; you can't prepare for success. The only way you can prepare yourself is working hard and doing your best at every audition, at every opportunity you get. - Millie Bobbie Brown

If you get an impulse in a scene, no matter how wrong it seems, follow the impulse. It might be something and if it ain't — take two. - Jack Nicholson

The difference between a hero and a coward is one step sideways. - Gene Hackman

There is no trick to writing an unbelievable love story. A heartbreaking scene or real dialogue. All you need is to tell the truth. It's always heartbreaking. - Ethan Hawke

The basic quality that any great story must have is a story hat illustrates the human condition. - William Shatner

---

I think you should take your job seriously, but not yourself. That is the best combination. - Judi Dench

---

Giving voice to characters that have no voice - that's the great worth of what we do. - Meryl Streep

---

What keeps you confident in a healthy way is knowing that everyone else around you is going to support you and teach you and you're going ti learn from them. I just feel open to learning from people. - Elizabeth Olsen

---

A creative act is throwing yourself out into the unknown. The more you do that the more you grow as a person and artist. - Mark Ruffalo

---

People were confused by me, and at first I was auditioning for a lot of the crazy characters or the victim, someone who'd been attacked. Which is great, because usually those are the best acting roles. - Jessica Chastain

I went through this realization that acting, at its heart, is the ability to manipulate you own emotions. - Scarlett Johansson

You can change your fee. You can sit back, or you can go after your life and all that you want it to be. - Hilary Swank

After many years of self-flagellation, I've realized that being myself up doesn't get me anywhere. - Chris Pine

We're all here because of the power of a story well told. Sometimes, that's good enough. - France McDormand

Work hard. Don't quit. Be appreciative. Be grateful. Be respectful. Never complain. Always keep a sense of humor. - Michael Keaton

I'm an actor. Not a star. Stars are people who live in Hollywood and have heart-shaped swimming pools. - Al Pacino

I don't care if people think I'm an overactor... People who think that would call Van Gogh an overpainter. - Jim Carey

I'm a big believe in 'Never say never.' - Jim Parsons

You can't have an ego when you're an actor. A lot of actors have them, but in reality most of those people are just sensitive artists dying for a hug and a compliment. - Josh Brolin

I just sort of follow my bliss, so to speak. And then see where that takes me. - Zooey Deschanel

I really love comedy and weirdly enough, I love how my journey has ended up. I get to laugh all day long. - Anna Faris

When your passion and drive are bigger than your fears, you just dive in. - Viola Davis

Everything I've donnas purpose and has been passionate and has been executed in the best way that I knew how. Maybe that's not the perfect way... But it's the best way I knew how to do it. - Julia Roberts

So many actors get caught up in their technique, and be to be honest, I see it really getting in the way. I see them forcing things. I definitely do my best work when I'm free of that. - Gerard Butler

Doubt is a killer. You just have to know who you are and what you stand for. - Jennifer Lopez

If you know you're going to fail, then fail gloriously. - Cate Blanchett

Don't be afraid to fail. It's not the end of the world, and in many ways, it's the first step towards something and getting better at it. - Jon Hamm

I've always thought Prince Charming in 'Cinderella' was the most boring role; I'd rather be the Wicked Witch. - Jude Law

Whenever I'm acting, it's everything. If I'm researching a role, I'm completely consumed in that. In between action and cut, I live in this suspended time. - Abbie Cornish

You live once and life is wonderful, so eat the damned red velvet cake. - Emma Stone

When I get logical, and don't trust my instincts - that's when I get in trouble. - Angelina Jolie

I'm a true believe in karma. You get what you give, whether it's bad or good. - Sandra Bullock

Don't feel stupid if you don't like what everyone else pretends to love. - Emma Watson

I've learned it's not really important not to limit yourself. You can do whatever you really love to do, no matter what it is. - Ryan Gosling

Know your lines. Really, just get that over with. Because once you learn your lines, then you can kind of settle in to all the other moments in the scene. - Leonardo Di Caprio

Acting is really about having the courage to fail in front of people. - Adam Driver

When we live our lives everyday, we're met by opportunities, and most of us don't even recognize them. - Scarlett Johansson

Actors are agents of change. A film, a piece of theater, a piece of music, or a book can make a difference. It can change the world. - Alan Rickman

The number one rule of acting is - 'do not seek approval from the audience.' People don't realize that. You can't do stuff to get applause. You have to live in the turret. - Chadwick Boseman

I think imperfections are important, just as mistakes are important. You only get to be good by making mistakes, and you only get to be real by being imperfect. - Julianne Moore

Acting is not rocket science... it is an art form. What you are doing is illuminating humanity. - Viola Davis

Keep moving forward. Don't be frustrated when your path gets messy. Because it will get messy. You'll fall and you'll fail along the way, wildly. Embrace the mess. - Octavia Spencer

Be in the moment. Period. Just be there... You've just got to let go. If it happens it happens. If it doesn't it doesn't. Whatever you do is okay. Just be truthful, honest, real and that's all you can ask for. - Robert De Niro

I think there was something in me from a young age that was not worried about success, but was worried about becoming a better actor. - Paul Dano

Acting is something different to everybody. I just know that tif you watch an actor or actress getting better and better, I think that's them just getting to know themselves better and better. - Cameron Diaz

What are the aspects of yourself that line up with the character? You magnify those, and the ones that don't match up you kind of kick to the curb. - Jeff Bridges

Never let yourself be defined by how you look. Never do that because (your career) will be over soon, and you won't develop.... So, if people go on and on about how you look, you have to challenge it. You can't just take it in, you have to challenge it. - Emma Thompson

Acting deals with very delicate emotions. It's not putting up a mask. Each time an actor acts he does not hide; he exposes himself. - Rodney Dangerfield

Being present is the actor's job. Being aware of your body, in space, and the emotions that are occurring inside, is essential. Well, quite simply, the more aware one is of yourself, of your surroundings, of other people - the more likely you are to respond truthfully. - Sandra Oh

One of the things that I like about acting is that, in a funny way, I come back to myself. - Bill Murray

Nothing is impossible. Even the word itself says I'm Possible. - Audrey Hepburn

You only live once, you don't want your tombstone to read: Played it safe. - Rosario Dawson

Involve yourself everyday. Work hard and figure out how to love acting all day, every day. It's getting into a made-up situation and making it good and making it real and just playing, just practicing and playing. Like the musicians that I played piano with: they never expect to be rich or famous, but they, for the sheer joy of it all, play every day, all day. - Jeff Goldblum

If you risk nothing, then you risk everything. - Geena Davis

To grasp the full significance of life is the actor's duty, to interpret it is his problem, and it express it his dedication. - Marlon Brando

Acting isn't a game of pretend. It's an exercise in being real. - Sidney Poitier

Being an actor is like being some kind of detective where you're on the search for a secret that will unlock the character. - Philip Seymour Hoffman

The gratification comes in the doing, not in the results. - James Dean

It dawned on me that acting was what I wanted to do with my life. Nothing had ever touched my heart like acting did. - Hugh Jackman

Art is good for my soul precisely because it reminds me that we have souls in the first place. - Tilda Swinton

Don't pretend to know everything. I've been blessed to work with a lot of veteran actors and I soak up lessons from them like a sponge. - Michael B. Jordan

I have come to appreciate the low points, and now hopefully I'll get to enjoy some of the highs, because you can't really know what sweet tastes like unless you know the sour. - Ke Huy Quan

All I would tell people is to hold on to what was individual about themselves, not to allow their ambition for success to cause them to try to imitate the success of others. You've got to find it on your own terms. - Harrison Ford

Your only job as an artist is to put the truth out there into the world. - Viola Davis

Without wonder and insight acting is just a business. With it, it becomes creation. - Bette Davis

---

I always want to know what I'm capable of. I want to reach out as far as I can. - Rami Malek

---

Be so good they can't ignore you. - Steve Martin

As enactor I have ideas, but things should always be fluid. You should always be ready to follow an instinct. Something might reveal itself on the day. - Michael Fassbender

---

Acting is a form of self-expression, it's not becoming someone else, and it's not playing make believe; it's about using the fiction of being someone else to express something about yourself. - Maggie Gyllenhaal

---

Be willing to fall flat on your face. And be in an unknown place. If you're doing that, you're probably growing. - Don Cheadle

I mean honestly I look at acting like it's my job to disappear. The best acting is invisible. - Michael Shannon

---

What sets you apart can feel like a burden, but it's not. A lot of the time it's what makes you great. - Emma Stone

---

Goals on the road to achievement cannot be achieved without discipline and consistency. - Denzel Washington

---

When I wasn't getting acting jobs all the time that I liked, I was writing and writing. - Helen Hunt

---

Artists don't need permission to work. - Chadwick Boseman

Step out of the history that tis holding you back. Step into the new story you are willing to create. - Oprah Winfrey

---

It will never be perfect, but perfect is overrated. Perfect is boring. - Tina Fey

---

Knowing is not enough, we must apply. Willing is not enough, we must do. - Bruce Lee

Everybody has to know for themselves what they're capable of. - Daniel Day Lewis

I think the most liberating things I did early on was to free myself from any concern with my looks as they pertained to my work. - Meryl Streep

Acting is not about being famous. It's about exploring the human soul. - Annette Benning

Acting is really about having the courage to fail in front of people. - Adam Driver

You've gotta believe in yourself, and you just have to work harder than you've ever worked at anything before in your life. And if you keep doing that and keep believing in yourself, great things do happen. - Kate McKinnon

The most exciting acting tends to happen in roles you never thought you could play. - John Lithgow

Portray the world for what it is, and you will find truth. - John Boyega

The more you enrich your life, the more enriched you'll be as an actor. - Kate Winslet

Relax. Just relax and have fun doing what you're doing. Don't worry so much about being results oriented. Just commit yourself to the moment. - John Goodman

In the end, some of your greatest pains, become your greatest strengths. - Drew Barrymore

When I connect to my soul, project it into another character and then bring it to the stage or to a film - it's always been for me the great joy of acting. It's been as if my soul leaps out of my body and is able to be free and dance around. - Kyra Sedgwick

What moves me in art is how we question who we are as people. - Ralph Fiennes

I am where I am because I believe in all possibilities. - Whoopi Goldberg

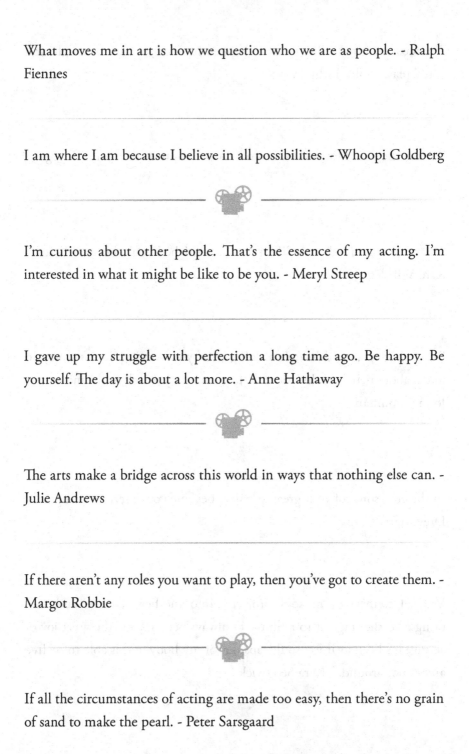

I'm curious about other people. That's the essence of my acting. I'm interested in what it might be like to be you. - Meryl Streep

I gave up my struggle with perfection a long time ago. Be happy. Be yourself. The day is about a lot more. - Anne Hathaway

The arts make a bridge across this world in ways that nothing else can. - Julie Andrews

If there aren't any roles you want to play, then you've got to create them. - Margot Robbie

If all the circumstances of acting are made too easy, then there's no grain of sand to make the pearl. - Peter Sarsgaard

Never, ever let anyone tell you what you can and can't do. Prove the cynics wrong. Pity them for they have no imagination. The sky's the limit. Your sky. Your limit. Now. Let's dance. - Tom Hiddleston

My desire to become an actor really early on was that I wanted to communicate something to reflect something back to the audience. For me that was powerful, I think that was more powerful. I think that was more important than being in the centre of the stage. To communicate something. - Matt Dillon

Be conscious of how long the journey is, be patient, push yourself, persevere and always be working on your craft while waiting for your break. - Mahershala Ali

I say luck is when an opportunity comes along and you're prepared for it. - Denzel Washington

I remember a long time ago, a theatre professor said that the definition of acting is 'living believably under an imaginary set of circumstances.' Living, not acting. You have to live. You re that guy. - John Krasinski

Life is what's important. Walking, houses, family, birth and pain and joy. Acting is just waiting for the custard pie. - Katherine Hepburn

Just let the wardrobe do the acting. - Jack Nicholson

When we are kids, we play, we think, we dream but as an adult we slow down very quickly. No matter what stage they are in life, people sound't stop dreaming. They should thrive on. - Idris Elba

If you really do want to be an actor who can satisfy himself and his audience, you need to be vulnerable. - Jack Lemmon

With any part you play there is a certain amount of yourself in it.There has to be, otherwise, it's not acting. It's lying. - Johnny Depp

My first Love was acting. I went to Sidney Poitier films as a kid. I sat in the theater and dreamed of being an actor. - Carl Weathers

I love acting because it's the space where dreams can be realized. Fantasy comes to life and there are no limitations on what's possible. - Jessica Alba

Use the difficulty. - Sir Michael Caine

People who eat with their mouth open should be punched in the face. - Kevin Hart

---

Honesty isn't enough for me. That becomes very boring. If you can convince people what you're doing is real and it's also bigger than life... that's exciting. - Gene Hackman

---

Always be a first-rate version of yourself instead of a second-rate version of somebody else. - Judy Garland

---

Without wonder and insight, acting is just a business. With it, it becomes creation. - Bette Davis

---

It's amazing what you can get if you quietly, clearly and authoritatively demand it. - Meryl Streep

I'm slow to pick things up. Everybody always seems to know more than I do. - Christopher Lloyd

---

To be an actor, a true actor, you have to be brokenhearted. - Shia Labeouf

---

I never act. I simply bring out the real animal that's in me. - William Dafoe

---

It's got to do with putting yourself in other people's shoes and seeing how far you cna come to truly understand them. I like the empathy that comes from acting. - Christian Bale

---

Acting should be bigger than life. Scripts should be bigger than life. It should all be bigger than life. - Bette Davis

---

If you get a chance to act in a room that somebody else has paid rent for, then you're given a free chance to practice your craft. - Phillip Seymour Hoffman

You have to be totally tough to deal with all those times when you're being turned down, and then really soft in order to access you character's emotions. - Felicity Jones

The actual work requires the same discipline and passion as any job you love doing, be is as a very good pipe fitter or a highly creative artist. - Tom Hanks

I'm curious about other people. That's the essence of my acting. I'm interested in what it would be like to be you. - Meryl Streep

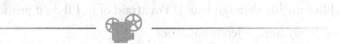

My job is usually to express emotion as freely as possible. - Meryl Streep

Honesty isn't enough for me. That becomes very boring. If you can convince people what you'e doing is real and it's also bigger than life - that's exciting. - Gene Hackman

If you really do want to be an actor who can satisfy himself and his audience, you need to be vulnerable. - Jack Lemmon

I think you self emerges more clearly over time. - Meryl Streep

---

You're not going there to get a job. YOu're going there to present what you do. - Bryan Cranston

---

Goals on the road to achievement cannot be achieved without discipline and consistency. - Denzel Washington

---

I live my life through fear. If I'm afraid of it, I'll do it just so I'm not afraid of it anymore. - Jeremy Renner

---

Don't take yourself too seriously. Know when to laugh at yourself, and find a way to laugh at obstacles that inevitably present themselves. - Halle Berry

---

One thing I've learned is be comfortable in your skin, and more importantly, be comfortable in your shoes. - Octavia Spencer

---

YOU have to be totally tough to deal with all those times when you're being turned down, and then really soft in order to access your character's emotions. - Felicity Jones

I'm continually trying to make choices that put me against my own comfort zone. As long as you're uncomfortable, it means you're growing. - Ashton Kutcher

The struggles along the way are only meant to shape you for your purpose. - Chadwick Boseman

I never took Ana acting class, so I've made all my mistakes on film. - Heath Ledger

My approach to acting is the 'let's pretend' school of acting. - Harrison Ford

You often meet your fate on the road you take to avoid it. - Goldie Hawn

Don't aspire to make a living; aspire to make a difference. - Denzel Washington

Life is very interesting… in the end, some of your greatest pains become your greatest strengths. - Drew Barrymore

---

If you're an actor, even a successful one, you're still waiting for the phone to ring. - Kevin Bacon

If all the circumstances of acting are made too easy, then there's no grain of sand ot make it a pearl. - Peter Sarasgaard

---

It's important to say that the more challenging scene is, in a way, the more fun it is because the more of my job I get to do. - Daniel Radcliffe

I've always thought of acting as more than an exercise in empathy, which is not not to be confused with sympathy. You're trying to get inside a certain emotional reality or motivational reality and try and figure out what that's about so you can represent it. - Edward Norton

---

I would love to have an ocean of love right now. That said, the number one rule of acting is, 'Do not seek approval from the audience.' People don't realize that. You can't do stuff to get applause. You have to live in the truth. - Chadwick Boseman

Acting has given me a way to channel my angst. I feel like an overweight, pimply faced kid a lot fo the time - and finding a way to access that insecurity, and put it towards something creative is incredibly rewarding. I feel very lucky. - Ryan Reynolds

It's got to do with putting yourself in other people's shoes and seeing how far you cna come to truly understand them. I like the empathy that comes from acting. - Christian Bale

If only we built gyms for kindness, where we worked on our compassion, our empathy, our patience, along with our bodies. - Marlon Brando

I'm so fortunate, it's ridiculous. - Norman Reedus

Pretending to be other people is my game and that to me is the essence of the whole business of acting. - John Hurt

My art, like my acting, is a profound expression of poetic license. - Adam West

Being an actor in Hollywood involves lots of things beyond acting. Charm really helps. - Pierce Brosnan

Acting is experience with something sweet behind it. - Humphrey Bogart

Acting is a childlike thing. To act well, you have to be childlike in order to free yourself. - Laurence Fishburne

I love eating because it's a bit of an escape. It gives you the ability to reinvent yourself. They say that acting is the shy man's revenge. - Hayden Christianson

I'm just starting to scratch the surface of what really makes me happy and it's taken me a while to admit that acting like a little child and being a jerk and punk is fun. - Leonardo DiCaprio

I'm still insecure, but when I first started acting, I was really insecure. I glared at a lot of people. I assumed everyone hated me. Somehow that scowl has turned into an acting career. - Norman Reedus

That's what I learned form the great actors that I work with. Stillness. That's all and that's the hardest thing. - Morgan Freeman

I was terrorized by the emotional requirements of being an actor. Acting is like letting your pants down; you're exposed. - Paul Newman

I remember a long time ago, a theater professor said that the definition of acting is 'lying believably under an imaginary set of circumstances.' Living not eating. You have to lie. You re that guy. - John Krasinski

Work was never about wanting fame or money. I never thought about that. I loved getting the job, going to rehearsal, playing someone else, hanging around with a bunch of actors. I needed that, the way you need water. - Sarah Jessica Parker

You're only given a little spark of madness. You mustn't lost it. - Robin Williams

Once in a while I experience an emotion on stage that is so gut wrenching, so heart-stopping, that I could weep with gratitude and joy. The feeling

catches and magnifies so rapidly that it threatens to engulf me. - Julie
Andrews

All my characters are me. I'm not a good enough actor to become a
character. I hear about actors who become the role and I think 'I wonder
what that feels like.' Because for me, they're all me. - Ryan Gosling

I like the character roles. Somewhere back there I really came to the
conclusion in my mind that the difference between acting and stardom was
major. And that if you become a star, people are going to go to se you. If
you remain an actor, they're going to go see the story you're in. - Morgan
Freeman

An actor must interpret life, and in order to do so must be willing to accept
all the experiences life has to offer. In fact, in fact he must seek out more
of life than life puts at his feet. - James Dean

Acting isn't really a creative profession. It's an interpretative one. - Paul
Newman

There's so much emphasis on Daniel Day-Lewis and his process, which is appropriately his won. But I was just blown away by his generosity as an actor the the just naturally commands focus on the set. - Adam Driver

There is such a thing as my kind of actor, and how well they pull of my dialogue is a very, very important part of it. - Quentin Tarantino

Maybe other people will try to limit me but I don't limit myself. - Jim Carey

The exciting part of acting, I don't know how else to explain it, are those moments when surprise yourself. - Tom Cruise

I'm happy everyday. - Bruce Willis

One of the things I like about acting is that, in a funny way, I come back to myself. - Bill Murray

Acting is the great answer to my loneliness that I have found. - Claire Danes

The most beautiful thing you can wear is confidence. - Blake Lively

---

And in a world without heroes, as the movie trailer voice-over guy might say, the slightly awkward can be slightly cool. - Adam Brody

---

When an actor plays a scene exactly the way a director orders, it isn't acting. It's following instructions. Anyone with the physical qualifications can do that. - James Dean

---

A good director creates an environment, which gives the actor the encouragement to fly. Kevin Bacon

---

If I get rejected for a part, I pick myself up and say 'OK not today, maybe tomorrow I'll get this other part or something. - Liam Neeson

---

My approach to acting is the 'let's pretend' school of acting. - Harrison Ford

Old age is no place for sissies. - Bette Davis

———————————— 🎥 ————————————

Working with amazing people, you continue to learn and develop yourself, as an actor and as a person. - Josh Hutcheson

It's easy to become very self-critical when you're an actor. Then you get critiqued by the critics. Whether you agree with them or not, people are passing judgement. - Keanu Reeves

———————————— 🎥 ————————————

Being a good actor isn't easy. Being a man is even harder. I want to be both before I'm done. - James Dean

I'd like to be remembered as a guy who tried… tried to be part of his times, tried to help people communicate with one another, tried to find some decency in his own life, tried to extend himself as a human being. Someone who isn't complacent, who doesn't cop out. - Paul Newman

———————————— 🎥 ————————————

I love that spirit that makes people do things that they probably shouldn't do. - Johnny Knoxville

You are the writer of your life. - Sean Patrick Flannery

With any part you play, there is a certain amount of yourself in it. There has to be, otherwise it's just not acting. It's lying. - Johnny Depp

---

The harder you try, the better the impression you set on the people around you. - Tom Holland

---

I'm not interested in becoming a bigger star, I'm not interested in being the wealthiest guy in the world. I'm fine, I love acting, and I want to do it for the rest of my life. - Seth Green

---

Acting allows me to explore new worlds, to discover characters by delving into their lives, and ultimately to become someone else entirely. - Pierce Brosnan

---

The whole things about acting, the draw for me, is the opportunity to do things you don't get to do in real life. - Benjamin Bratt

The better I am at observing moments in life, the better I'll be at showing them in my acting. - Oscar Isaac

---

A wise man can learn more from a foolish question than a fool can learn from a wise answer. - Bruce Lee

---

We each have a star, all we have to do is find it. Once you do, everyone who sees it will be blinded. - DMX

Great theatre is about challenging how we think and encouraging us to fantasize about a world we aspire to. - William Dafoe

---

Don't listen to anyone who doesn't know how to dream. - Liza Minnelli

---

I pretty much operate on adrenaline and ignorance. - Johnny Knoxville

---

There are two kinds of people in this world. 'I' people and 'we' people. I've always tried to be a 'we' person. - Clint Eastwood

---

If you love life, don't waste time. For time is what life is made up of. - Bruce Lee

There is something inherently tough about Americans. They will accept defeat. - Ron Howard

---

I think the thing to do is enjoy the ride while you're on it. - Johnny Depp

---

I gravitate towards sort of broken characters who try to be better people.- Matthew Perry

---

I think acting has helped me come out of my shell because when I play a character, I can't be self conscious. - Joan Cusack

---

It's what still excites me most about acting: Letting your imagination go places it's never been before. There's nothing better than that. - Robin Wright

---

If you're trying to learn how to act from a class, you're analyzing the teachers' movements and their intricacies, and it becomes like a pantomime of you wanting to be them, and that's wrong. Literature is an easier way to study acting, because then you can take any kind of spin. It's your own imaginations and your own version of it. - Shia Labeouf

Acting is sort of an extension of childhood. You get to play all of these roles and have so much fun. Playing an athlete would be so cool. Or where you get to shoot guns, ride horses. I wouldn't turn down any of that - - Jon Hamm

For me, becoming a man had a lot to do with learning communication, and I learned about that by acting. - Adam Driver

One good thing about acting is films is that it's good therapy. - Denzel Washington

The nerds are the ones that make the films and do loads of other really cool stuff in their life. - Daniel Radcliffe

You have to cherish things in a different way when you know the clock is ticking. You are under pressure. - Chadwick Boseman

Doing nothing is very hard work to do... you never know when you're finished. - Leslie Nielsen

Acting engenders and harbours qualities that are best left way behind in adolescent. - Carrie Fisher

Life is a great big canvas; throw all the paint you can at it. - Danny Kaye

With any part you play there is a certain amount of yourself in it. There has to be, otherwise it's just not acting. It's lying. - Johnny Depp

A day without laughter is a day wasted. - Charlie Chaplin

I learn a lot with actors that I don't think are good. Every experience shapes you. - Kristen Stewart

You have to do everything you can. You have to work your hardest. And if you do, if you stay positive, then you have a shot at a silver lining. - Bradley Cooper

Most actors don't really have a director's sensibility. They have an actor's sensibility. - Jodie Foster

The foundation of any great movie is the performances. A great script can only be elevated by talented actors who bring the words to life. - Steven Spielberg

Actors are agents of change. A film, a piece of theatre, a piece of music or a book can make a difference. It can change the world. Alan Rickman

You want to make sure that you're putting your passion into things that you care about so that it's actually refuelling that well rather than just taking from you... I never want to fall out of love with my art. - Anya Taylor-Joy

Many people worry so much about managing their careers, but rarely spend half that much energy managing their lives. I want to make my life, not just my job, the best it can be. The rest will work itself out. - Reese Witherspoon

The acting thing is so beyond my control. Acting isn't mine. You're like a tiny piece in this big, corporate mechanism that needs chemistry and divine intervention. - Sandra Bullock

Art is good for my soul precisely because it reminds me that we have souls in the first place. - Tilda Swinton

The best actors instinctively feel out what the other actors need, and they just accommodate it. - Christopher Nolan

I don't need to be a lead, I don't need to have a big part in a film. I will literally play any part as long as the character's interesting or I'm working with interesting people. - David Bautista

Everybody needs a passion. That's what keeps like interesting. If you live without passion, you can go through life without leaving any footprints. - Betty White

I realize as an actor I put myself in situations that feel masochistic because I am so uncomfortable. But then I also think, I'm so lucky to get to do what I do. It's such a gift to have this job. So in some sense, it's like my penance.

I'm supposed to be uncomfortable. I'm supposed to do things that don't feel good sometimes. It makes it worth it. - Jessica Chastain

There's no reason to be afraid here, just go for it. That's the line I am constantly saying to myself when I'm writing and acting. - Phoebe Waller-Bridge

The stuff that really makes me happy is getting to do the art. It's not the red carpet, and it's not the box office, and it's not any of these external things. The external things, they're like drugs. They'll make you happy for a second, and then you just want more. You're feeding an empty hole, and it's never really satisfying. Shift your perspective and say, 'actually, what matters to me is: I'm expressing myself.'" - Joseph Gordon- Levitt

I enjoy acting now more than I ever have. I've had lots of difficult times when I was younger, but that was all tied up with thwarted ambition. It's hard being a young actor, because you don't realize until later that it's only ever about doing the work. - Brian Cox

I would say there's no real style of acting. It's almost like a mixed martial art. It can be whatever you want it to be. You can combine, you can create your own Feet Kune Do with acting. Don't get trapped in a style. Don't get trapped in Naturalism, and be open to your dreams. Your imagination is your most important tool, and there are ways to augment your imagination, healthy ways to augment your imagination so that you're not necessarily doing, you're being. - Nicholas Cage

My father could have been a great comedian but he didn't believe that that was possible for him, so he made a conservative choice. Instead he got a safe job as an accountant and when I was 12 years old he was let go from that safe job, and our family had to do whatever we could to survive. I learned many great lessons from my father. Not the least of which was that: You can fail at what you don't want. So you might as well take a chance on doing what you love. - Jim Carey

I think I've always been fuelled by rejection. It only made me want it more, because I think I just had that thing inside of me that's like: 'I wanna be in the club that I'm not in' or whatever that that is; 'I want the thing that I can't have, or the thing that I don't have.' And if you tell me that I'm not good enough, I'll jut find a way to prove you wrong somehow. - Aubrey Plaza

Great people do things before they're ready. They do things before they know they can do it. Doing what you're afraid of, getting out of your comfort zone, taking risks like that - that's what life is. You might be really good. You might find out something about yourself that's really special and if you're not good, who cares? You tried something. Now you know something about yourself. - Amy Poehler

I think failure is a brilliant thing. It teaches you a lot of stuff, you end up coming up with better ideas. When you fail at things. I think what's really great is learning to embrace bad creative experiences. - Taki Waititi

Sometimes a dream almost whispers... it never shouts. Very hard to hear. So you have to, every day of your lives, be ready to hear what whispers in your ear. - Stephen Spielberg

I think you have to be present. This life is yours. But if you're not present, it's wasted. Time waits for no one. When we're born, we age na then we die, and God forbid, we die before we have lived our lives. So we have t be present in whatever universe, in whatever life, because if you give up on being present, then you give up on your life. - Michelle Yeoh

If you're going to define me properly, you must think in terms of my failures as well as my successes. - Harrison Ford

Whenever we reach what we think are the boundaries of our endurance, you know ten minutes later you're thinking: I could have done that - like in any athletic pursuit - I could have gone further than that; I could have jumped higher. - Daniel Day-Lewis

So long as I'm a working actor, I can improve. I want to work with people that frighten me and excite me, and characters that I don't believe I'm the best person for the part but I'm still gonna try any waylay. - Anne Hathaway

Where I think the most work needs to be done is behind the camera, not in front of it. - Denzel Washington

The number one rule of acting is: Do not seek approval from the audience. People don't realize that. You can't do stuff to get applause. You have to live in the truth. - Chadwick Boseman

It was only when I realized how actors have the power to move people that I decided to pursue acting as career. - Cate Blanchett

When you're playing the good guy, you want to find the dirty parts - and when you're playing the bad guy, you want to find the vulnerability. - Patrick Wilson

I hope that I'm always struggling, really, you develop when you're struggling. When you're struggling, you get stronger. - Andrew Garfield

Challenge yourself: It's the only path which leads to growth. - Morgan Freeman

I'm not Brad Pitt or George Clooney. Those guys walk into a room and the room changes. I think there's something more.... Not average, but everyman about me. - Matt Damon

Remember just because you hit bottom, doesn't mean you have to stay there. - Robert Downey Jr.

The way you behave withe everybody is more important than the work you do.Generosity, kindness and patience willet you so far. That's the biggest lesson I've learned. - Jake Gyllenhaal

I wanted my dad ot be proud of me, and I fell into acting because there wasn't anything else I could do, and in it I found a discipline that I wanted to keep coming back to, that I love and I learn about every day. - Tom Hardy

It's got to do with putting yourself in other people's shoes and seeing how far you can come to truly understand them. I like the empathy that comes from acting. Christian Bale

Acting is a very personally process. It has to do with expressing your own personality, and discovering the character you're playing through your own experience - so we're all different. - Ian Mckellen

There is a part of your brain that has to stop when you're acting. You have to be in the moment and dare to fly. Words can't be on your mind. - Penelope Cruz

ABOUT THE AUTHOR

Douglas Vermeeren is an actor, producer, director and stuntman. Appearing in over fifty movies and television shows he started acting at the age of seven. He is also the producer of 5 of the top personal development films which have been translated into more than 26 languages worldwide.

Printed in the United States
by Baker & Taylor Publisher Services

Printed in the United States
by Baker & Taylor Publisher Services